Barn Raising

by Nancy Furstinger

Illustrated by Ashley Wolff

Scott Foresman
is an imprint of

Glenview, Illinois • Boston, Massachusetts • Mesa, Arizona
Shoreview, Minnesota • Upper Saddle River, New Jersey

Illustrations
Ashley Wolff

ISBN 13: 978-0-328-39371-8
ISBN 10: 0-328-39371-1

1 2 3 4 5 6 7 8 9 10 V010 17 16 15 14 13 12 11 10 09 08

The town barn was built long ago.
It is time to build a new one.
The whole town wakes up early to help.

People work together.
First, they measure and cut enough wood.
Next, they drill holes for posts.

People work together.
Some workers nail bars of wood
above the posts.
The word for a bar like this is *beam*.

The workers leave at noon.
They head toward tables in the shade.
Friends have made a picnic!

The workers finish the walls after lunch.
At last, they hang the door.
The barn looks great!

People work together to fill the barn.
Horses enter their home.
Workers stack bales of hay.
Everyone is ready to rest!